Lines from a Canvas

Lines from a Canvas

POEMS

Jacob Miller

DALKEY ARCHIVE PRESS

Cover painting by J. B. Miller
Cover design by E. V. Svetova
Photograph by Alexander Ag
Cover composition by Danielle Collins

First edition, 2016

Library of Congress Cataloging-in-Publication Data
Names: Miller, Jacob, author.
Title: Lines from a canvas : poems / Jacob Miller.
Description: First edition. | Victoria, TX : Dalkey Archive Press, 2016.
Identifiers: LCCN 2016011483 | ISBN 9781628971378 (pbk. : alk. paper)
Classification: LCC PS3613.I53725 A6 2016 | DDC 811/.6--dc23
LC record available at https://lccn.loc.gov/2016011483

Copyright registration TXu 1-995-221

ILLINOIS
ARTS
COUNCIL
AGENCY

Partially funded by a grant by the Illinois Arts Council, a state agency

www.dalkeyarchive.com

Victoria, TX / McLean, IL / Dublin

Dalkey Archive Press publications are, in part, made possible through the support of the University of Houston-Victoria and its programs in creative writing, publishing, and translation.

Printed on permanent/durable acid-free paper

Acknowledgements

Some of these poems first appeared, in somewhat different form, in *World Order, The Michigan Daily, The Guild House Journal, Bayou, The Absolute Journal, The Empyrea Anthology*, and *Rising Star Journal.* The Free Verse Libretto "Manhattan in Charcoal" first appeared in print as a folio pamphlet with the CD of the opera "Manhattan in Charcoal" from *Composers Concordance Records.* The poem "Blues from an Airport Bar" first came out, in an earlier version with music, on the CD "Song Cycles," also from *Composers Concordance Records.*

My special thanks go to the New York Foundation for the Arts and the Concordia Foundation, which made it possible for me to complete this collection.

To my friend and fellow poet, Toby Roberts, my thanks for (as Robert Hayden once put it, as Henry James would have said) "watching with me" through the years.

For Rita & my children, Hayden, Alexander & Naomi
& John O'Brien,
a friend in a desert where I'd grown to expect only sand.

Contents

Lines from a Canvas

My unfinished mesh
    leans against a wall,
    itches for the scratch
    of a Boar's hair brush,
the zinc glisten with liquin and beeswax.

Three or four paintings
from earlier efforts
    that were abandoned,
    now brood, just
    beneath my surface,
concealed by revisions.

Overhead,
a light-bulb shakes a clenched fist,
its arm an exposed wire.

I don't want
to be seen though,
    as I am—
        muddled, imperfect,
a sheet started from woven Hemp,
stretched to a thin wooden frame.

God only knows
what painting might next touch me.

I'm never completed,
just a place to search—
    I should've been the floor
    of a boxing ring or,
just as easily, I could've been a sail—

All's the same search,
   same sweating fight,
   same wind,
   same streak of oil,
   gauze of last light—
the same search for texture.

On the Elusive Quality of Bridges

From the roof of my high-rise,
I can see
    the bridges'
        creased sleeves,
        stretched iron rods,
        piano strings.

The proof is there,
    right before my eyes,
    where the sky's
        gauze
        bandages all.

So, I am quite certain—
    No, I'm convinced—
    the bridges exist.
Indeed, each night, the evidence
    appears the same.

It's incontrovertible
    when the G.W.,
    the Triborough,
    the 59th Street,
    and the Brooklyn's
    strapped on lights begin
    to sputter and blush
    luminous splashes on
the Hudson and East rivers' skin.

But each morning,
    back on the street,
when I search

round the rims
of our island,
I can't find a bridge
anywhere.

And it's no use
asking for directions.
They all end the same, with
disappointed expectations.

Despite faithfully following
every suggested
twist and turn—
Despite enduring traffic
hour after hour—
the bridges still elude me.

And it seems, there's nothing
to satisfy
the absurd absence
of bridges.

I know they exist,
those extended
paths between
our edges,
the hidden high routes
that facilitate transporting
one to another place,
the elevated passageways
that connect
one body to another—

Hell, I'm perfectly prepared
to pay whatever the toll is—
yet, I'm still searching,
struggling to find
a way to cross over.

Odysseus at the Veterans Hospital

'Kirke, who pilots me upon this journey?
No man has ever sailed to the land of Death?'
—Homer

Beyond the hospital, a beach,
       a strip of sand where my past
       twists in brine, shines in sea glass
and floats with empty beer cans.

I don't know what I'm still doing here.

Mostly, I listen to the waves bitch,
       watch how they shrug and
           then collapse—
listen to my stale cigarettes
sputter and hiss questions I can't guess.
Mostly, I'm hooked on the head nurse,
       Circe, who dispenses the meds.

After the war,
       being at sea for so long,
       I didn't give a fuck,
       my legs still wobbled,
           and I was stuck—
           homesick and blue—
until Circe started cutting up
           pharmaceutical blow
that leveled me, anchored me.

Also, to her credit,
       when she spread her legs,
       she reminded me of
       what can return after battles
           and emptied bottles,

namely, lust—
the one thing in the war
I'd not entirely lost.

So, here I've stayed,
and whatever's filled me
with my few clear thoughts,
I've filled this Circe
with the notions an ocean tossed.

But she's also had her way with me:
watching her parsing the powder
into neat lines,
then licking and dipping one of
her delicate fingertips
into the snow,
the way she rubs my gums numb,
I'm struck dumb.

Here, the nurse becomes a Goddess.
Here, a cursed mortal—blessed.
Here is how
I snort my way to release,
and every threat
is swallowed
with an acrid drip at my throat.

And so it's been for a year—
in the high tide of her bed,
harboring my imagination,
my exposed hull held fast—
I didn't notice when her sex
started to smell like an obligation.

But today,
after I pulled out of Circe,
I thought of my wife,

thought of my son,
and knew I'd had it,
that I had to head back to Ithaca.

But to be perfectly honest,
I'm a weak and selfish shit;
I like getting laid;
I like getting high.

And so I haven't stayed,
to be a hero or defeat a lie
and not because Fate
played a fucked-up joke—

In truth,
I've stayed for the pussy
and I've stayed for the coke.

I even forgot about the other vets
who first took to this place
like pigs to slop—
my crawling crew, who Circe
had left to grunt and mewl in the mud—
but today, somehow my mood
finally changed, my eyes opened.

The psych. ward here,
known as the flight deck,
is where I told Circe
I had to go back to my wife,
my son, my old life.

Then, despite her white uniform,
with her arms waving, feet
stamping, as if in a storm,
she looked less a nurse
and more like a patient.

"Well," she spat at last,
        face aflame,
"I think you should go to Hell!"
Then, she even gave me directions.

And now,
        I'm tempted by her suggestion
        seeing as, since the war,
            at my best,
though I know she's no kind intention,
I'm inclined to trust myself less.

Along the shore
        my last ship's bow
        slaps up and down on its
            stubbled hull,
        and I may damn Circe,
        but where else will I go
if not, as she put it, straight to Hell?

Homage to Golda, 1946

A cough
after a wet cigarette
     is all
Golda can offer the Doctor
when he stops
     speaking,
     tugs on his beard,
     and steps
toward her.

"Did you hear me?" he asks.
No reply:
     she hugs her bag,
     feels ill.

Here's
where sister Esther
     is locked up;
the diagnosis,
     schizophrenia,
does not translate
     into Yiddish.

Here, the doors are bolted.
My grandmother's looked
     for an exit
     past the shuffling
bathrobed shoulders.

Tzivia,
     her cousin,
is somewhere in Palestine;

she'd lost it when
they started to
            empty the ghetto,
robbed by the Poles
who'd promised to sell guns.
She got some
            from others anyway.

In Warsaw,
at sixteen,
Tzivia lost it, then
            killed
                        Jewish collaborators,
            killed
                        Nazis,
            killed
                        more Nazis,
            killed
                        more Nazis—
Then escaped through the sewers,
            made her way to the Promised Land,
            killed
                        British soldiers,
            killed
                        Arabs.

"Did you hear me?
 Do you understand what I just said?"

Golda doesn't hear the doctor,
            just hugs her bag tighter.

What else?
Half-sisters in Argentina,
sister Sara in Brooklyn,
            useless, in a haze,
            spending winters
swimming off Coney Island.

"So," Golda turns, asks,
        as if the doctor is
in the hall on a horse,
        high in the saddle,
        waving a saber,
"you are Cossack?"

But the Doctor doesn't
        understand her Russian,
just tilts his head, stares at her.
        And my grandmother
knows that look.

Nature is Roman & Mirrors Rome

Nature is Roman, & mirrors Rome...
There are entrails of sacrifice to guess at wars,
Slaves to be silent, stones to build.
                                    —Osip Mandelstam, 1914

1.

Which way to enter Rome,
        when all roads lead here?
Which road to take
        if not the one my people took,
entering the seat of the Empire as slaves,
ghettoed on the other side of the Tiber,
        brought across the river only
            when of use,
            to serve Senators,
            grovel before Centurions,
or a Coliseum needed building?

Which road though for a Jew of the Pagan poets?
        Which road for such a confused exile?
Where Catullus, Propertius, Ovid and Virgil
                        once strolled,
        vendors now hawk postcards to tourists.

All roads lead to the same place but which is mine?

2.

Back here, at the Antica Pensione,
          pacing while scribbling in my mind
                    these very lines,
alive with nature and aloud for all of Rome,
          a lovely Sophia groans,
                    in the room next to mine,
seeking shelter beneath Lucio's shoulder.

Back here, at the Antica Pensione,
                    a dive suitable for
the cataloging of Nero's debaucheries,
          I am compelled to write free-verse,
          returning to Rome in this life,
                    a freed slave,
                    I refuse to be ruled.

          I drink with *il Padronne di Casa*,
a well-fed man with crooked teeth who inquires,
"Is New York, *Professori*, much like *Roma?*"

3.

Which way to enter Rome,
        home to the descendants
        of the destroyers of Solomon's Temple,
        home to a Vatican that suffered
            selective blindness
        to Spain's Inquisition and Germany's
            "Final Solution"?

Which road admits the Rome that
        made a Michelangelo live hand-to-mouth,
        the Rome that bruised a Bernini into brilliance,
        the Rome that elevated and subjugated,
            celebrated and denigrated,
            her artists and poets alike?

Which road roared for Benito,
        even as he seduced Pound
        into coming around,
        into believing the time had arrived
        for poets again to be cherished—
            the outcome, madness, St. Elizabeth's,
        should've been obvious, clear,
            foreseeable from the start?

4.

There is too much of Rome
            for one city to contain it;
      no wonder it spilled over maps,
         gulped neighbors
and thought to govern the globe.

Roman is our nature,
      a nature that craves to battle,
      seeks truth in a bottle,
      damns the conquered,
      drives the conqueror,
         harbors artists,
         havens sculptors,
         hovers with poets,
and revolves over its own red-tiled rooftops.

There is too much passion
         and too much hate here
      for me to understand the ease
        with which I am
so entirely at home in this place.

In a bar near the Trevi Fountain,
        I'm killing an afternoon,
      downing one *Grappa* after another,
      until, somewhere in the dust of dusk,
        I hear an old man telling me,
forse in un' altra vita I was Roman.

5.

By the time I'm staggering back
          to the Antica Pensione,
     a siren slices the night,
          bending its note
               as it turns a corner.

In a crowded piazza,
          a carabinieri stares at pigeons,
               as the Party's anthem,
          supported by an ambitious tenor,
               fills the Roman night,
                    resounds off ruins.

Beyond the piazza,
               I enter a dark alley, not
                    wide enough
                    for two men
                    to walk side
                         by side—

And it's here I give up on discerning
                    the right road—
               as if there could ever be
               one right road for Rome.

Then a woman's voice,
          two words, a question,
          penetrating the darkness,
          hammers the message home,
                    "Sei solo"?

What the Rain Has to Say

He now sits
       unnaturally still
in a chair by the window,
watching as drops of rain
          steal
      slowly down the pane
         of glass.

The night stretches
      quiet as a caesura.
He can't move but is moved.
He'd like to say something,
       but is not sure of
         the words.

The rain tears
      from the fabric of clouds.
         The rain's tears
turn the sky into a broken faucet.

And on a statue in the piazza,
      where no pane
      separates the face it
      offers the elements,
in the mist and streetlight—

      on the lone statue,
the only one left to listen
to what the rain has to say—
      stone cheeks glisten.

Maybe There's Too Much Manhattan

Maybe there's too much Manhattan.
        Here is where I started
                and always return.
        More than Moscow,
                here the city spills
over the lip of each glass I drink from,
        over the slate bar of each dive
where centuries hide and come alive.

Of course there's too much Manhattan.
        It floods
                the boathouse in the park
and agitates the currents of the Hudson.

Here, even more than Rome,
        is the most resilient
                        town on the globe.
Here, around the clock,
the reach of inconsistent architecture
        defines, in its varying lines,
the brittle logic of History as injury.

Yes, it's Manhattan, not Paris,
        that truly delivers
        lectures in traffic,
        writes and rehearses
        plays on busses,
and composes symphonies of secrets
to be performed on steel subways.

Spilling from
        Lincoln Center's fountain,

spilling over
      the Bethesda in the park,
it makes streets and avenues slippery.
      Here, horses bolt from carriages
lined up in front of the Plaza.

Of course, there's too much Manhattan
        for one island.
Yet, here is where
      I can write and say fuck cash.

And even if most of my poems are trash—
syllables that merely scratch and thrash
        across a page—
here is where my bantering verses first
        started to swim fast
        and my metric feet,
     perhaps even years from now,
        might still be kicking,
leaving their own slight splash.

Lightning-lit in a Storm

Again, I return to what's left:
    streets and lines
    of buildings and statues
nodding in shadows.

What else remains?

I ran into my childhood friend,
    after so many years,
    downtown.
—found him shivering under
    a store's canopy,
    looking sketchy,
    dodging the rain.

When we were young,
    I'd looked up to him,
    hung on his words—
He was going to be an important artist;
I would be the scribbler of unnoticed poems.

After I saw him in that storm,
    he had me up to his room
    at the Chelsea Hotel,
        and casual,
    like he's making a cup of tea,
    he sparked a flame
        from his Zippo,
          and left it
    licking beneath an old spoon,
while he chewed a belt round
his arm's bicep.

As a smile played at his lips,
        a sudden stab of lightning
        illuminated the room.

Later,
after he stopped nodding,
        he was hurling paint at
        a canvas on a clothesline,
        while the storm outside
continued raging.

"I'm still painting," he said,
        "but the work of a junky
        who's still breathing,
        the bastards dismiss.
It's only when
        the exact same work
        comes from a dead artist
they decide it's worth something."

After that,
        I tried to calm him down
        as he paced and scratched,
        getting himself worked up,
        flinching at claps of thunder,
but then I left,
just got out of there—

Next day though,
        feeling guilty,
        I went back.

His door was unlocked
        and I found him
        frozen on his side
        on the couch in his boxers—

Plain as day,
    the last fix
        still stood—
           a hypodermic
              Tower of Pisa—
                leaning in his arm.

Meantime,
his torso appeared painted with
    the half he was laying on
    cerulean blue, and his skin
on the other side zinc white.

"Overcome," is a weak word
    for feeling numb,
    when mind-blank fear
    strikes us dumb,
unable to speak to the moment.

Standing in the doorway of that room,
    I wondered who had failed here:
    him, me, or our generation?

Then, after a moment, recalling him
        lightning-lit in that storm,
I closed the door.

Engine

There was the usual
      warbling of words about the soul,
      then the shovel coughing into soil—
            the hoarse voice of the shovel,
            followed by clods of mud
pummeling the coffin.

Then, when the digging stopped,
            in the grammar of death,
            it was as if for a period—
or wasn't it just a comma?

Later, the sky started out stoned
      in the dust of dusk
            with a gray light,
                  until night
      brought on a darkness that
grew thick as a coma.

Later still, perhaps an engine began,
      again recalled what was felt—
            a light mist
      breathing across a field,
the overgrown grass on one's legs.

Outside the cemetery,
      life stretched for sleep,
      cried cries that glimmered
      like a promising thought,
then faded in the back of a throat.

Maybe the mourners whispered "Amen,"
but who knows if an engine
will still accelerate,
throttle through curves,
continue after it sputters,
stalls, and won't turn over again?

Judaean Entry

Hiking outside of Jerusalem,
    I walk where I should not
    until an Arab and his camel
    stumble up to me.

The man looks at me—
    a look worth a thousand words—
and I'm not expecting to
    heal age-old hatreds,
    just pay a toll,
so I offer him American cigarettes.

Suddenly, quicker
than I thought he could move,
    he grabs the tobacco,
    hands me a brick of Hashish,
    then resumes his path,
leaning into the hill.

"Hey, Ishmael," I want to call out,
    "don't you recognize me?
    It's me, Isaac.
We buried our father, Abraham,
together at the cave of Machpelah."

But I say nothing,
    find a clearing,
        light a fire
        with dry, crisp twigs,
and boil a pot of tea with the Hash.

Night, cough
    and crackle of embers.

And across the Judaean hills,
        sky starts spilling stars,
        as I make my pillow
                from a stone,
        wondering if History,
        in her own shaky skin,
has any tips on how to be alone.

Shooting Darts in London

Beside the old oak bar
    in the Chelsea Pub,
    we were the young Yanks,
    with our most precious asset,
        our inexperience,
leading us by our longings.

Waiting to shoot darts,
    engine already revving,
    you were the girl
    rubbing her cheek against
the shoulder of my leather jacket.

"Can we go?"

"No, let's have another pint."

And we did stay,
    drank too much,
    even eventually
        shot darts
surprisingly half-decently,
    you better than me,
    despite throwing
        in the blind,
half-dancing, half-spinning,
    half-out of your mind.

Then you fell into my arms,
    your eyes blinking hope,
    lashes fluttering promise—

"I'll always love you," you said,
"and I'll never leave you."

And even today,
        I can hear your words,
        like distant music
fading down a hall.

Of course, I knew it was all
                nonsense,
        even then, even when
        I saw nothing ahead
                but our end.

It was just two years later,
        you left over coffee—

"Oh, this coffee's good,"
        you politely remarked,
"Can I have another cup
        and a divorce?"

"Why?"

"Because I'm thirsty."

"No, not the coffee, goddamnit—
        the divorce?"

You squinted at that—
        perhaps saw again
        the cork bull's-eye—
then let the feathered dart fly.

"I thought it'd be fun
        being married to a poet—
        really, I did—
but it isn't much fun at all."

The Ghost of Persius

Every man jack has an ass's ears! That's my secret;
that's my joke. Slight as it is, I wouldn't sell it for
all your Iliads.
—Aules Persius Flaccus 54 A.D.

Tonight I was haunted by the ghost of Persius.
        He followed after me,
            speaking kindly of Cornutus the Stoic
and warning me of the fraternity of Bards.

His tired voice warbled in the wind
        as he told me I am wrong, misled,
            that nothing has changed,
            that for all our thoughts aloft
            poets will always be left
                by those we love.

Even in my dream,
        I tried to shake him, walk away,
            but Persius persisted, insisted
                (following me)
            that still, poets are all so many
        fat cows with foul breath to be milked
for the emotions others have the sense to resist.

In the end, he wouldn't shut up,
        but went on, saying how we are sent
        to the page to scribble perceived
            episodes of flight and ascent
        that will always be received
            as the same exaggerated cant
mumbled through the nose of a well-fed poet.

Finally, wanting to be rid of him and rest,
     I pretended to agree, play nice,
   even said how Poesy is a wicked vice,
   a weak habit that leads many to slice
       their wrists.

Then the gray, wrinkled ghost stood
     beside me, nodding slowly.

But he was silent when I asked of his
     own quarrel with Reason,
   of his intimacy with that demure animal
   called "Wisdom".

At the moment I expected an answer,
   he became evasive, began to resist,
   and it was then, I said *screw rest*
   and suddenly wanted to pursue it.

But then I thought,
     what is wrong with me?
     Who, in their right mind,
   wants to argue with dead poets?
Even if this may be part of the job
   any half-decent poet signs up for,
   just maybe I'm not up to the job.

And so I kept my mouth shut,
listened to Persius mutter, *shit*,
   then just watched him turn away
with a bitter smile playing at his lips.

Perhaps it was
   the fatigue of language,
   the weary scraping
   of words against throat.

No matter, I won't be indiscreet,
       I thought, to my nocturnal guest.
       Instead, perhaps it is best
to respect the privacy of ghosts.

In Memory of Robert Hayden

(1913-1980)

1.

Dead of winter.
      Dark of night.
I'm walking through
this Michigan cemetery
      looking for your headstone,
      noticing how each grave
      presents its own page
from the same unfinished book.

Call what's written here
      a work in progress,
      where each generation
offers its own chapter.

Call it
a composition from the hereafter,
      where
      the final editor's busy,
proofing the galleys.

But as bad
as the publishing industry is,
      you can't stop
      the submission of new pages,
scribbled on manuscripts of snow.

2.

When I find your grave,
        pausing
                at the corner
                of a thought,
I begin reading
        as a tree's shadow
        becomes your hospital bed
        and,
        in a tangle of branches
                        shivering,
I see your stitches and tubes.

In the end,
        you spoke of
        finally feeling
        you could put down
in black and white
                exactly what
        eluded you for so long,
then grieved over
        all that would be
                left undone.

In the din
        of underwater bone-cave,
        you shrugged superbly,
                whispering
        how the poems that
                wash over paper
offer only parts.

In the end,
        you said,
        death drinks the rest,
swallowing all that's unwritten.

3.

"What else is certain," you asked,
        "and not banal?"
Then stared
        at the hospital ceiling,
a cork panel.

"We ride bicycles,
        read books,
        attend parties
        we'd rather avoid,
        wear carefully laundered clothes,
        resist questions,
        assume somber expressions,
fall hard and tough in and out of love…"

Then you blinked,
        coughed,
caught your breath,

        "Ah, this world I have loved
                and so lovingly hated…"

4.

I'm watching
    a squirrel,
    in search of scraps,
    squat
        then scamper
over graves.

Up above,
    the moon, draped by clouds,
        crowds
the sky silver.

Standing by your grave,
    dizzy with
the quick miracle of confusion
    we, the survivors,
      call *grief*,
I still long to talk with you, Robert.

That life's faltering, fragile internal
    experience has a chance
    of offering something eternal
    in the language's dance
    across a page, is what you
    spoke of, defying bounds—

    while others rattled on about
    the competitive merits
of real estate versus stocks and bonds.

But who can I talk with now?

5.

"Oh, master now love's instruments—"
      you wrote,
"know that love has chosen you."

And never shied
      from the search,
      the service to the page,
you taught as
      complex and simple
      in its one rule—
           it never lied.

I recall you fighting
      till the end
      to defeat the flaws,
insisting each line
must read effortless,
      like no fuss was made
          in its invention,
despite a lifetime of effort.

An explorer,
      you scaled in verse
          the cliffs of uncertainty,
          climbing stanzas
          without a rest
      to wrestle with life and death.

6.

I can see you striking a stick match,
        lighting your pipe,
adjusted your Coke-bottle glasses,
        then offering a sad nod.

Robert, I'm shivering
        in this winter cemetery,
but grateful your lines survive,
        identifying
        what is right,
        what you called fundamental,
        where to begin,
        how to hold what is human
up to the light.

Nearby,
        a train of flatbeds pulls
Fords fresh from the River Rouge plant.

The Michigan sky is still silver,
        only now it's snowing too,
        offering,
for each of your crafted cadences,
        nature's scansion notes
        on the wind's page.

What is crucial remains with me:

        you were right,
                the flaws must be forgiven,
        just as the poems
                forgive the poet
                for being human,
        exploring the shared experience
                in isolation,
and scribbling a last line.

August 26, 1997

My earliest Siberia was suburbia,
        the American variety of the ordinary,
        stretching manicured lawns where
I raked leaves and waited to hit the city.

This was when the smell of burning leaves
                still brought Autumn to the air.

Next:
winters I'd hoist snow from
        the gravel-toothed paths of Connecticut,
                attend the shovel's cough into slush,
before snow blowers killed a kid's business.

Year round,
        with my father,
        a handsome butcher and decorated veteran,
I cut down sides of red meat
        from metal hooks that toughed
leather shoulders on New York's docks.

After that,
        half a nation away,
        in rusted flatbed trucks,
I crossed Michigan flatlands
        moving near and far,
        till time and snow
        covered my tracks,
delivering kegs of beer
to aspiring alcoholics.

Later,
I moved to *bella Italia*—
 climbed the Alps
   till my breath was thin,
     my voice hoarse.

Today I'm forty.
Same as the number of years
my people were lost
 in the desert,
 scorched,
 dry-throated nomads,
   meandering.

So,
does this mean
 the Promised Land
 is just ahead,
   or waiting around
     the next corner?

It seems,
I may be of the generation
 that isn't allowed
to enter the land of milk and honey.

What have I done?

I've painted mediocre canvases,
 scribbled
  my share of inadequate lines.
In a pinch,
 with devoted Socialists,
 I dined on horse.

In short,

I've done nothing spectacular.

Mostly,
relationships have reduced me—
    left me
        winded,
            seeing an oasis
where there was none—
    left my expectations loitering,
        slipping in sand.

Still,
a student of the unattainable
in all I see,
    I'm thankful for this short life,
    and almost scared
    to leave what's known
in the familiar dizziness of the desert.

The Voice from a Pontiac V8

Closing time at
　　　my father's meat market,
dusk to sawdust turns locks.
　　　Moments later,
the old man guns the Pontiac,
　　　looks mad,
　　　　　puffs on his Tiparillo.

An hour earlier,
I was cleaning a cutting block—
　　　wire brush and salt to
　　　blood and blonde wood—
when this guy starts in,
　　　calls my old man a
　　　cheap fucking Jew,
then talks how
　　　Hitler had the right idea,
　　　but didn't finish the job.

And all this cause
　　　my old man doesn't let
　　　this guy pass a bad check.

My father weighs
　　　the cleaver in his hand,
　　　studies the sharpness of the blade,
　　　but sets it down,
steps out from behind the counter,
then lays the son-of-a-bitch out
　　　with one punch,
　　　　　lifted him off his feet
　　　　　and dropped him flat.

Now the Pontiac is moving
        and the old man's muttering
        about Uncle Yakov.

"The *arbeiten* never made him *frei*.
        A lime pit is all he got,
        so you don't forget it.
They wanted to kill all of us,
        but just didn't get to…"

When he stops talking,
        I look up.
I'm still a boy,
        not tall enough yet
        to work the counter.
The first words are
        still the hardest,
           a test.

"But what did Uncle Yakov do wrong?
        Why'd they want to kill us?"

This is where I learn
        not all questions are
        easier for grown-ups.

This is the way
        my father bites his lip.
This is the way
        my father tells me, *sha.*
This is the way
        my old man punches the dashboard,
           then shakes his fist.

This is how a Pontiac
        twists and slips

fast into the sea of traffic.

This is where
    the swart engine
gravels its metal throat.

Papa Karamazov & Alyosha

The father,
        already in his cups,
           several shredded sheets to the wind,
              rises from his armchair,
greets the young woman,
        then seeing his youngest son,
        Alyosha, not leaving,
           glares at him,
reaches for his belt, then changes his mind.

"Forgive me, son.
        I am a dreadful ass of a man,
           not even an ass—
        that is giving myself too much—
        I am not so much as a beast of burden;
they, at least, serve a purpose, while I serve none.

Quite simply, though I pray, try to be humble
        and long to change my ways,
        I am still a hopeless liar.
Why even now, I am such a liar I, myself,
cannot say if a single word I've just uttered
        was at all truly heartfelt.
        But you already know that—

        Hah! I know you do.
And yet you still forgive me, don't you, dear boy?"

Alyosha nods, even as he ponders the sordid
        details of his family,
        ponders, once again, why Zosima

sent him into the world.

Suddenly, a balloon
               floats
through the young man's head,
                        diagonally
        from nape to temple;
        it pauses,
        drops
then starts back.

Meanwhile,
        knees weak,
        shoulders wavering,
his father,
        sagging as he is,
gives up the effort of standing,
        falls in his chair,
knuckles an arthritic paw
to his vodka
        on the side table,
leers at the young woman,
        and waves his son
            out of the room
without looking at him.

Alyosha notices
        the yellow nails
        on his father's pudgy fingers—
notices the bags under
the old man's excited eyes.

"Go,"
the old man finally shouts.

And so the young man moves,
        despite a nagging uncertainty

as to exactly where
or even
in what direction
he should go.

The Texture of Tears

. . . at fifty I have learnt that beyond words
is the disfiguring exile of divorce.
—Derek Walcott

I was born with
      bad eyes, muddled vision,
      bad motor skills,
            cried in the crib
            with conviction,
            with an extra trembling
                  in little hands,
     and a longing to
     hold or be held.

It was about the same
      when I got married.

Today, I live on my own,
      separated from my children—
but what's really changed?

I still can't see straight—
      relationships blur,
            angles confound me.
I still have fingers that
      don't cooperate—
            matches shiver
      each time I fire up a smoke.

So, what's really changed?

I used to be there to hear

when my children were
crying in the crib
    with conviction,
    with staggered breath,
        hoping to be heard—
        hoping to be held—
and I'd the needful gift of proximity
    permitting me to respond.

Now, I can only remember
    hearing their cries,
      seeing the pools in their eyes,
seeing the trembling of their lower lips.

I can only recall how I'd bend over the crib
      and kiss their little faces,
      each mirroring a miniature
        something of me.

Now, I can only remember wiping
    their tears with my fingers
    when they were still weeping,
      remember and miss
    the taste of salt on their cheeks
      in the midst of each kiss.

Now, I can only remember how,
      myself a veteran of crying,
all too familiar with the texture of tears,
      when I held them
    and rocked my children in my arms,
    it was enough to comfort them,
      to stop their tears,
if I let them know they were not alone,
if I let them know their father was home.

When Open Arms Could Still Define a Home

I return to what I recall:
    marble fingers
        moving
as she played her flute.

Or was it
    alabaster lips
        moving
as she spoke of her father,
a truck driver in Detroit?

Me, music or words,
marble or alabaster—
    it was all one,
    it was all some
    magic she'd spun,
letting me hold and hear
her breathing statue near.

Of course, I was certain
    I'd wasted my life
till I met her that night.

Later,
after she moved in,
    I watched her,
        extended,
        on tiptoes,
take down the black blankets
    which I,
    lacking curtains,
had nailed over the windows.

After that, the midday sun
　　　used to hit
　　　the four-poster bed,
just as we so often did.

In those days,
　　　what was felt was
　　　worn on our sleeves,
sewn into the invincible fabric
of being young and in love—

It was a time, so long ago now,
　　　when the one thing known
　　　was, if I held her fast,
open arms could
still define a home.

Lines on the Death of "Free Love"

We can share the women, we can share the wine.
—fr. "Jack Straw," Grateful Dead, 1971

When my best friend walked out of our
  rain written world,
   with hardly a word,
he smoked my last American cigarette.

We'd met in London after he went wild,
   out of his mind,
  left his lover in Michigan
   and followed mine
across the Atlantic.

He wanted to take her to Paris, he said,
  but she'd turned him down,
   so now he was sad,
sorry my Emma wasn't going with him
  to some stoned vision of a home
   on the Left Bank.

He thought I'd understand his twist
  on how a true Romantic had
  to go to Paris, as an artist,
  with another man's woman,
and no means of support to paint.

And I almost saw his point,
  but held onto my girl.

When he left London,
  he muttered,
  "Screw the game of being

a whole-wheat hippie with wings.
        I'll find me a gal named Fifi
        by next week and be reading
her Robinson's *Man Against the Sky*."

But in the end,
        the way Time can fly—
        the unpredictable velocity,
        the rising and falling altitudes,
            not to mention,
        our own changeable attitudes—

Of course, he never found his Fifi
        and today, all these years later,
        Emma isn't with either of us.

Instead,
        we've both grown gray,
        hitting the road each day,
            each of us lugging
our own memory of that one brunette
in our separate beat-up suitcases,
            packed as a regret.

Excerpt from a 2007 interview with Bob Weir on the origins of lyrics to "Jack Straw":

"I had just read *Of Mice and Men* . . . I was completely smitten by that story . . . and this story emerged between me and Hunter about these two guys on the lam . . . ne'er-do-wells . . . I always felt very strange about the roar that would emerge at the lines *we can share the women, we can share the wine*. In fact, that attitude led our pair of ne'er-do-wells onto a path of self-destruction. Regardless, this song frequently brought a shot of adrenaline to a show, and its message of friendship gone astray and lives wasted might make us pause. And hey—it pays to read Steinbeck!"

Song of an American Generation

With drug-fueled dreams
in torn and faded jeans,
swearing off suits and ties,
swearing off the lure of the almighty buck,
swearing how we'd never grow old or give a fuck
        about such garbage as two car garages—
We were going to be different.

Dancing, deliciously drunk, down
        dimly lit streets and dimly lit loves,
we still somehow managed to stand
        against the war in Vietnam,
        and believed in King's dream,
    when *Peace* and *Equality* was seen
        as just around the corner—
We were going to change the world.

Later, with bloodshot eyes and dilated pupils,
        we stayed awake for endless days,
        debated inspired theories of nonsense
                in an acid haze,
        skinny-dipped in lakes of wild ideas,
        streaked naked in streets paved with fears,
        paved slick and glistening wet with ecstatic tears—
Still determined to be different.

But now, it's another century:
        the age of another generation's lust,
            and those of us who are not entirely lost—
        who can still hear our youth like an old song
        played with a dusty needle tracking along
                the static of our past on vinyl—

we are finding the song of our generation fading,
both the melody and lyrics receding.

Yet, last night, eating a late dinner
                in a crowded west side café,
      I saw a white haired couple
                groping on the sidewalk on Broadway.

The old lady was rubbing her arthritic paw
                up and down the crotch
                of the old man's corduroys,
                while he was busy in her sweater—

All this, in front of the crowded café.

As people walked by the amorous couple,
                most pretended not to notice,
                as we New Yorkers tend to,
                but others were laughing, snickering.

As for myself, I wasn't sure how to respond,
                but then I realized I admired them—
                these two white-haired remnants of a
                      once promising generation—
                for this may be exactly where we end up,
                despite the loftiest ambitions and
                      invincible experiments of our youth,
                white-haired and groping in the dark
                      on the crowded sidewalk of life,
                ignored or ridiculed but, if we are lucky,
                      still able to hold a loved one close.

A Matter of Taste

That first time we kissed,
      when I tasted her tongue,
      I tasted the short-quick
         day of being young.

It still seems moments ago—
      I entered her
         shower and
    carried her to
    then lay her
on the kitchen table.

But no,
it was years ago.

Gone are the tastes
      of her skin's heat,
      of her cheek's flush,
      of the rise and
acceleration of pulse,
      of her waist's grind,
      of the arch of her spine.

Whatever happened to that
      shaking kitchen table?

With the taste of her lips,
      I could taste
         each irregular breath
she'd catch and take.

But no,
it was years ago.
    And today,
        such precious tastes
might as well be
        in Gibbon's,
        in Thucydides,
or any other ancient history—

I am almost
embarrassed,
        at my age,
to mention such matters.

Yet,
why should I
        pretend
I don't recall?

Today,
        with her gone,
        and me alone,
            watching
        my beard grow
        from gray to white,
what should I savor?

The Nature of Flight

—for my father, 1924–2016

1.

Let the engines roar.
Let the engines throb.
It's 1945, and the war is a job
where my father's F4U soars
through a storm called History.

Pushing forward on the stick,
     the young Marine pilot
          dives through a thick
cloud after a Zero skimming the Pacific,
     off the coast of Okinawa.

Dropping behind the Zero as it
     makes for the USS Franklin—
my father's breathing, fast and thin,
his thoughts, but not his plane,
          going into a spin—
he squints through his goggles to see
     the tail of the *kamikaze*.

Only fifty feet behind the Zero,
     his wings almost kissing
     the waves kicking
up, he opens fire with his Brownings.

But after he takes out the Zero,
     his plane's hit by flak,
so my father pulls the stick back,
     climbs into a black
cloud, and makes for his carrier.

Only later, when he drops down—
        his gull wings inclining
into a crooked-slant-angling tilt—
his carrier's bouncing in Buckner Bay,
        and he recalls being a boy,
thinks of his mother and sister,
thinks of a toy boat in a bathtub.

His wingman takes
        the first approach,
but his friend's plane misses the deck,
        slams into the bouncing hull,
then everything goes to hell.

In a sort of trance,
a daze following the waves' wild dance,
with flames licking my father's wings—
        flying half-blind from the smoke,
        coughing in his Corsair, a wreck
somehow traveling toward the deck,
despite his wings being strafed—
        he touches down and is safe.

The century called for more,
        above the South Pacific,
        in the engine's roar,
        in the engine's throb,
Manhood ducking in a cockpit,
the angle of descent determined.

2.

Somewhere in the blurred distortion
of decades, the fucked-up contortion
      of Time, the fighter pilot
      becomes a brooding butcher,
      grounded behind a counter.

At first, it must've seemed deranged
to have his flight suit exchanged
           for a bloody apron.

But with *his* war over, he's suddenly
      just another civilian,
      a small town merchant,
      watching how his life
can be reduced to sharpening a knife
      and nodding at customers.

Yet, when my brothers and I roll in,
talk of the war is off-limits, though he
still expects us to stand in formation,
          to stand at attention,
      to be perfect little *grunts*.

Eventually though, it's 1971,
      and ever the imperfect son,
      with my hair grown long,
      dancing to my own song,
relishing my own passage of Time,
I'm ready to commit a heinous crime—

It's here the words in my throat climb
      to my lips, ready to soar,
         needing to explore
my father's take on *my* generation's war.

Of course, to him, I'm well aware,
I'm a skinny, teen-aged pain in the ass,
but something in me still needs to ask,
and I figure the worst my words can do
                    is take off and crash.

When I approach the old flyboy
he's working on his Canadian Club,
and I'm still high, having achieved
          a decent altitude from the joint
          I just smoked in the backyard,
so maybe we're both feeling numb
          when I bring up Vietnam.

"I get it, Dad, Japan attacked—
          America had to respond,
          but this is different—"

In the store,
          he'd shoulder a side of beef
          over three hundred pounds
          without flinching, but here
the unbearable weight of words
          makes the old man grimace.

He finishes his drink in one pull,
          pours another full
          to the brim of his glass,
          then mutters at last,
blinking at me through his glass,
like I'm some annoying speck,
          how he's too tired to speak.

I had to accept, he didn't care to talk
          about his war or mine—
          that I was left to find
my own way, like learning to walk.

After that, the closest I came to my
        own taste of the nature of flight
        was not in an aerial dogfight
        off the coast of Okinawa,
        but when, after downing a bottle
of tequila, I was peaking on blotter acid
and, wringing the neck of my throttle,
        taking my motorcycle up to
one hundred miles an hour on a ride
        down a winding country road,
        ignoring, just driving over,
            the cavernous holes
I was hallucinating in the pavement.

Sure, I knew damn well I was flying,
but I can't really say that constitutes
        a battle scene or
        exactly who the enemy was,
except perhaps that pain in the ass kid
        who still hid in my own skin?

In the end, I wasn't tough,
but sobered up just long enough
        to see us leave Vietnam,
        and my old man tear his
  "Love It or Leave It"
bumper sticker off the Buick—
only to replace it with one reading:

"Not as lean, not as mean,
        but still a Marine."

3.

Again, there's the blurred distortion
of decades, only now it's that skinny,
       teen-aged pain in the ass
       whose turn it is to pass
through the fucked-up contortion of Time.

Suddenly, my tie-dye tee shirt long gone,
it's another century, it's 2001, and all
hell breaks loose when the Twin Towers fall.

On the morning of 9/11,
       after hearing the news,
neighbors rushed to grocery stores
       to stock up on supplies—
while I did my own version of the same,
       heading for the liquor store.

After that, armed for battle
       with a few bottles,
       along with other parents, I
headed to my boys' elementary school
       to bring my own sons home early.

On the walk uptown,
       my younger son looking south,
behind him, toward lower Manhattan,
pointed at the plumes of black clouds
       drifting toward us:
           "What's that, Papa?"

I recalled how my father blinked
       through his drink—
       Was he buying time to think,
or seeing me as an annoying speck,
or just uncertain of how to speak?

"It's only a storm," I lied, wanting to spare
          my sons having to be scared.
"Let's hustle now," I said, to maintain my lie,
          and avoid having to try
explain what was racing in my brain.
          I kept my voice calm—my words plain:
"We need to get home before it starts to rain."

But later, at home, seeing the news on TV,
          my sons wanted to know more:
               "Is this a war?"
And then, "Why do wars happen?"

In that moment, I suddenly understood,
          though flawed and inadequate, the
perversely perfect temptation of muttering,
          "I'm too tired to speak."

Looking back, I suppose
          I've done no better
               with my boys
          than my father did by me.

In fairness though,
when I needed the old flyboy,
          I was so far gone in my own
               stoned haze,
even if he had spoken in those days,
could I have made sense of his syllables?

But with my sons,
          I can't conveniently put
               my own inadequacies on them.

By the time they were in high school,
          their mother and I broke up,
and I was no longer there to field
the tough questions they never raised

on weekend visits.

So here I am tonight, up late,
        worrying that fathers and sons
might never find or utter the right words—
syllables that don't ache like sore muscles—
        the needful words to heal
a world that seems headed to hell.

The engines still roar—that's for damn sure.
The engines still throb, sadly.

But an old man myself now,
        an observer of multiple wars,
        an observer of multiple generations,
I cannot accept that there is not more
        to explain the insanity of war,
        or more, when we look back,
        to fill in the sad lack
        of satisfactory answers
        for fathers to offer their sons
to better understand the nature of flight.

Time Happens

Lately,
      I'm finding myself
      sitting with a glass of vodka,
then lifting my eyes suddenly,
      startled and certain
      someone's speaking to me,
          only to realize—
      after rubbing my eyes,
      after squinting,
      after wiping the sweat
      from my forehead
and scanning every inch of the room—
that no person has uttered a word to me
      but it is, in fact,
simply the drink that I've heard.

Maybe such sensitive hearing
      is not so common.
Maybe I should be worried.
But I'm convinced there's no
right or wrong as such things go.

Hell, I admit
      each conversation I have
         with my drink
tends to be one-sided and quite limited.

In fact,
      I can only confidently attest
      that my glass of vodka
lately utters two words.

It is always the same,
  the insidiously whispered refrain
I hear from the Russian remedy—
  the two words:
Time Happens.

A Line Forever Twisting North

Before I'm old enough
  to be left alone,
after my parents go to work,
  by morning's first light,
  I watch my *Zadee*
pouring vodka into his orange juice.

He scratches his beard,
  winks at me,
  downs the drink,
  wipes his lips
with his bathrobe sleeve.

And I want to talk
  about Mickey Mantle,
  but *Zadee's* talking
about the old country:

"Years before the Germans,
  there was the Tzar
what sent my oldest brother
  to Siberia,
  and my mother,
    oluva shalom,
  your great-grandmother,
who never complained to nobody,
wanted to visit him
  only, in them days,
  there was no train
  what went so far north."

"Yeah—so what'd she do *Zadee*?"

"Well, she says how
        without her first born son
        she's like
        a *Shabbos* candle with no wick,
then she left."

For a moment, I imagine
        a long walk,
        a wilderness of snow,
        a forest of ice and
a line forever twisting north.

"So what'd you do, *Zadee*?"

"Me,"
        he chokes the neck
        of the vodka bottle,
"in the words of Delmore Schwartz,
I come to America to be a Tzar myself."

Three Less One

All along
        the light was wrong,
                the storm,
sleet slapping avenue,
curtain slapping window.

December,
        the afternoon arranged
        my wife's arms
        in a web of wires,
                tubes—
        her winter of skin was
                sponged,
                swabbed.

Between contractions,
the nurse said,
                rest,
        then
        legs tightened,
                back arched,
for the next—

Eighteen hours later,
the nurse shook her head,
                looking from
the inactive fetal monitor
        to my wife's torso.

And here, I was
        useless, worthless,
a collection of gestures—

Despite the lofty
            assertions of Aristotle,
                  in the end,
a man can become no more
            than a pair of shoulders
            to ask about insurance.

It would have been a boy—a son
                  I could've come
            to know, watched grow.

But, he only knew her, his mother,
            in all those months
                  he grew inside her.

As for her, at the same time, she'd begun
            to already know him, our son,
                  with each kick,
                  each twist and turn,
each of his movements that moved her.

As for me—
            what was I but a voice
            that sometimes stepped
                  in and out of hearing?

In the end, I learned
            I know nothing
            and have no clear belief
            about how two people
            can align their grief.

Our plan,
            like all expectant parents,
            was to defy math and make
            one plus one equal three.

But afterwards,
    when she wouldn't
    look at me, it seemed we
    were no longer even two
    people—

        nothing added up—

What we were left with had been
    baffled by subtraction,
    and minus the boy, our son,
    we couldn't find an answer
        to three less one.

Blues from an Airport Bar

1.

Night throws in the towel
        with a cloud.
The brightness of stars
        retreats to gray cotton.
Her plane takes off,
        leaves the ground and
        lifts into the fog while
I grow wooden in the airport bar,
        ready to be hammered.

Just now, drinking's a shortcut
        into the fog,
        into her last location.
Meantime, the jukebox sings
        since my baby left me...

The blues work
        when all else is inadequate.
Anyway, this is where
        her image gets assessed
        best, in American music,
        when I'm getting soused
in the gray-blue haze of fog.

Given enough drinks, the mind sinks
        into the fog, stormy weather,
        and accepts that people change,
        and rarely together,
        rarely in alignment.

I thought I understood what was meant
        by the words *till death do we part*,
        that we each repeated like a parrot,
            but now suspect,
        until one draws one's last breath,
there's no decent words to define death.

2.

I set out to write Sonnets,
     but bar napkins can't handle
fourteen lines scribbled beside a candle.

Instead, I write one line:
     screw clarity anyway—
     it's my generation's song,
and has the virtue of not being too long.

We lived for the blues and
     nothing was wrong—
     notes drifted in the air.

It's late now as
     I order another drink.
     My throat is parched
as I try to steady my perch
     on this bar-stool.

Here, the beer stained floor leans
     toward the steel blue
     smoke above.

The jukebox blares:
     when she decided to leave,
all she said was she was done with love.

Once, we thought ourselves blessed,
     but at the boarding gate, after
     she wished me the best,
     then departed, I had to digest
in my life she was just a passing guest.

3.

I raise my glass to the fog
       hovering over the tarmac
      and toast the blue mist.
Here, while I'm hitting the bottle,
       thoughts can still throttle
down the runway of my mind
       and lift off:

What if, by some magic,
       she were to walk
into this bar right now to talk,
       to fill in that blank
         called the future?

Would I rub my eyes and blink,
       then just buy her a drink,
just ask what she's having,
       just pretend like it's plain
       there's no need to explain?

Or would I quote Catullus:
       So much for you, bitch—
       Now...whom will you kiss?
       And whose lips will you nibble?

In this airport bar,
       the nature of life is bare:
we are all transients, passing through,
killing time, listening to the blues.

Now the music rises.
       Now a note bends and
       twists into a groan.

Now my pen is filled
        with the ink of fog.

Damn the blues.
        Let these lines be burned.
        Let the music explode.

In this bar,
        a man's returned to his origin,
        stuck between the fog outside
and the fog within.

On School Training

Our fathers' war was hot,
    but, at eight years old,
    our war was cold
and, by a pond in the woods,
    a skinny kid
    with muddy sneakers,
all that mattered was
    catching a frog or
    triple-skipping a stone.

In school, they said
    America was *this*,
    and Russia was *that*,
but my grandpa talked like
    Boris on Bullwinkle,
even when telling me how
    Mother Russia was
    no mother to her Jews—

Still, English was not his or
    my mother's first language—
So what did that make my family?

Mostly, I didn't like school.

I recall practice air raids,
    how we'd crouch
    beneath our desks,
    and try to remain calm
while thinking about the bomb.

What might it be like,
        I wondered,
to go up in smoke?

Zadee whispered,
        across the kitchen table,
        how this was
the Nuclear Age,
        and *nicht fur dem kinder*
            to *fashtes*.

And I didn't *fashtes*,
        didn't understand,
        still don't,
        still wonder—

At age eight or eighty,
juggling assorted fears and doubts,
        catching frogs or
        catching a train
            of thought,
as the chalk on the blackboard blurs,
as the alarm from the firehouse blares,
watching or recalling how
        little Katy's skirt rode up
        when she ducked her head
            beneath her desk—

I still wonder,
        will I ever really leave school,
            will I ever stop
        searching for substance,
        searching for something certain,
        searching for some secure ground?

A Fight with the Boys

Brooding on blacktop,
    I'm walking alone,
    a kid kicking a stone,
    with a skull full of
    blonde Katy from school
who doesn't know I'm alive.

For her, I decide,
    I'll write my first lines:
        Roses are red,
        Violets are blue, etc.,
only it can't just be about flowers.

But then,
    the older boys start in on me.
"Hey kid,
why'd your people kill sweet Jesus?"

There's always more to it—
    one's father used to
    work at my old man's store,
but my father had to let him go—
    so the line comes out.

"I asked you a question!"

At nine,
answers are the hardest—
    sharp-edged syllables
        stick in the throat—

"Kid, I asked you a question:
    why'd you kill Jesus?"

Homer asked early,
     which of the gods was it
     that made them quarrel?

But, at nine,
     I haven't read Homer yet—
     and there's no running to
        the library in town
when the older boys knock me down.

After a boy finds himself on the ground
     getting kicked a while,
     more than just his back
        and ribs ache,
in his bones he learns how to hate.

So when they're laughing how
     "kikes got no stones,"
     my hand finds a rock and
        I get to my feet,
        ready to fight,
waving that rock in my hand.

Some boys can be
     throttled with words,
     other kids need a fist,
but it doesn't hurt to have a rock.

When the rock finds
     the loud mouth's face,
     the others step back fast,
and now no one's laughing.

Then I see his face,
     and I know it's bad.
Like beef bleeding red
     on the sawdust floor

of my father's store,
his white cheek pours.

And suddenly,
    across that street,
    I see where
lovely Katy from class stands,
    covering her mouth
with her little hands.

Literature is an Elderly Woman
in a Flannel Suit

*When Orpheus was gone, one Muse was yet haply
left, but when thou will perish, ah Literature, the
harp likewise shall cease; for until then there will
yet live some hope for a little fragment of the old
melodies.*

—Leontius

Tonight, Literature is wearing
    a flannel suit for dining out.
    It's winter now,
    in more ways than one,
and there's no need of snow to know it.

Once, she used to smack
    her lips at the smell of steaks
        and smoke.
Now she taps her plate with her fork.

Times have changed,
    the most innocent joke
    can be taken wrong and
    there's no pardoning mistakes—
    so like a modern and solid
citizen, she orders an organic salad.

Literature's suffered through centuries
    of writers who bore her,
    their Furies hounding them
    with their nagging compulsion
    to expose the old cast and crew
of exhausted emotions as if they were new.

But she still listens for what might be heard
        when those few leave the herd
and light the warm furnace of a phrase
        that might flash and catch a page.

Tonight though,
        she's out to eat and drink.
            What of it?
        Literature likes to drink.
        Syllables thirst for libations.

Now she studies
        the blonde, blue-eyed waitress
        and questions her own intentions—
how easy the young are to undress.

Literature had a weakness for men
        for ages that, of course,
                was unfair,
        but lately it's young women
            who set her on fire.

The waitress is thin, petite;
        she might even be discreet.
Her blonde tresses are tied up,
        exposing the nape of her neck.
What would it be to lie beside her,
        hold her, or just touch her
        young skin, follow the delicate
curves of her torso with her fingers?

As Literature finishes her drink,
        she waves the waitress over,
        orders another and thinks
how falling in love's still as easy as ever.

Literature is almost tempted to wink,

but then, catching her reflection
in a nearby mirror, shivers
and returns to herself, recalling
that to most she's beneath notice, not cute,
but just an elderly woman in a flannel suit.

fr. The Journal of Lucius Apuleius

Apuleius, author of The Golden Ass, *married an older, rich widow who later brought an action charging him with having won her love by means of magic. He afterwards journeyed through Africa giving philosophical lectures as one of the Sophists of the Empire.*

155 c.e.

Who, by the gods, will read this?
      Are you asking me? No one.
        So what?

After two days on my back,
      fighting a fever in Carthage,
      I've my own view of my affairs,
      beyond the ill-attended lectures
that ostensibly keep me here.

Let me begin by trying not to whine
      or look for a sign
to explain what I'm doing in this damn age.

Isn't it enough I had to endure
      the absurd accusations and drivel
      from my idiot in-laws?

Screw them!
As if Aemilia didn't know her own mind,
      taking in the first young stray
      she found stuck in the mud—
      half-crazed, damn near mad,
      with nowhere to turn, torn
        up inside,
having squandered my family's fortune—

It was clear she knew what she wanted,
  and I knew it wasn't a thirst for
  the finer subtleties of Philosophie.

I am sick of it all!
Even writing's now unpleasant, all's saying
  the same as an ass braying at roofs,
  dragging past path after path,
  page after page, beating your hoofs.

And what of *The Golden Ass*?
  It remains unread, collecting dust.
  I thought the premise sound,
  surely touching on universal ground:
Who of us hasn't been turned into an ass by love?

Still, my book was doomed from the start.
  What did I expect?
  That my work would ever be read?
  And what if it is?

They'll say, "Lucian's is better writ" or
  "Why's he messing about in Latin
  with what's better left in Greek?"

But fuck what people say!
  Right now, I am sick, most of all,
  of popular thought and the damn,
    stinking critics.
They might as well be deaf and dumb,
  for all their prancing about
  like they're oracles with a sense
    of what'll be sinking
    into posterity.

Both popular thought and the critics'
  pronouncements come,

like a drink from the public
fountain out of any village here,
with a wide assortment of infections.

Unhinged

The door creaks.
     The door moans.
          The rusted hinge is removed.

Everything they told you
in childhood was wrong.
They said,
     "Pursue your own song."
Earnest teachers, erudite scholars
     all agreed,
     children *must*,
in the words of a famous Fascist,
have some breath for beauty and the arts.

So they read them mountains of poetry.
Together
     they scaled the treacherous cliffs
          of obsolete textures,
               works on paper,
                    works on canvas.

Then the masters scratched their bellies,
     scratched their scalps—

Of course, they knew all along
     it was wrong,
          doomed from the start,
          where none dared
whisper of the world outside of school,
of the staggering work-a-day world
     where a wrinkled wad of dollars
     was enough to make them drool.

Meantime,
squinting through the fog,
        looking up to the tower of academia,
Poetry, Art, Music—
        all was sewn up,
        all defined by neatly distinct genres,
        all defined by
well-sanitized areas of specialization.

Here,
each thread of a thought
was bought and tangled tight
        to keep the outside unseen,
in fact, invisible—
        but who pulled the strings?

It's not as easy as
        the old cowboy movies suggest;
the bad guy
        does not always wear a black hat.

Nor is it
        only starched suits who,
                blinking behind wire glasses,
                pinching tightly knotted silk ties,
decide what is the acceptable aesthetic.

Still,
as for me,
        I'm ready,
        champing at my bit—

Let me bite the hand that
        doesn't feed me!
Let me rip the hinge
        from the door!
Let me explore
        the needful thing called *more*!

While the accountants and dentists
of our weary world
    pick their deductions,
    pick their crooked teeth,
every poet, musician and artist
    is another sailor
        harboring the swart ship
            of their disappointments.

Just try doing something different—
The door creaks.
    The door moans.
        The rusted hinge is removed—

Uncertainty flashes a perfect ass,
doubts glisten like shattered glass.

No matter,
it is the time of the unhinged!

Inhale structure;
    exhale deviation;
    let the music find its own location;
embrace obscurity;
    caress the obsolete;
become intimate with all that's incomplete—

From one millennium into the next,
I have scribbled my share
    of short and overlong lines,
    and watched all the signs,
            indented or
flush left,
    in free verse
or in hammering rhymes,
and it's plain what's called for—

There is no one exact way

to march syllables across a page
that alone defines an age—

The hinge must be removed from the door;
the door must be removed from the frame;
throw out the dreck that's all the same;
throw out what's tried and true.

In the end,
since solo sailing,
drenched in words,
takes a lifetime to never perfect,
no matter what mooring a poem
ties up to at the end of its voyage,
back on shore,
hiding in the heart's hollow home,
we'll all still be alone,
facing the same certain end.

Eyes may glimmer
through the gauze of night,
peer through the pool of assorted fears,
moisten,
water up,
but there will be no last,
lingering
tissue of a thought left
to wipe away
the tears.

Let the door creak.
Let the door moan.
Let the hinge splinter wood
as it's ripped from the frame.

It is the time of the unhinged!

MANHATTAN IN CHARCOAL

A Free Verse Libretto

Movement 1

(Narrator standing stage right.)

NARRATOR:
It's late when even the Village feels empty.
Drowsing curbside, plastic bags of garbage
lean against each other.
Mostly, the artist has been kicking a can
across the sidewalk, as the dark tan concrete
sweats rain near St. Mark's.
The can echoes, a metal cough, a scratch like
a stick of charcoal or a match struck—

But let me light a smoke,
startle the gray with sparks,
and get back to where this story starts.

(Narrator lights a cigarette.)

Earlier tonight, a line of cars twisted
down this street in the rain, while a tear made
its own line, twisting down Beatrice's cheek—
very Solomon like—*All is futile*, etc.

The artist knew she was sick of art and artists,
that she suspected him of loving another,
that she'd grown weary of watching him
pushing paint around on canvas,
or scratching at all hours with charcoal,
so he didn't press her to talk, just left.

*(Narrator exits stage right, light comes up on Artist and
Beatrice in loft. Center stage is a living room—stage left*

97

is the artist's work space/studio—both are standing beside
couch with conspicuous charcoal smudge on it.)

ARTIST:
 I see it. The charcoal smudge I left on our couch
 has caught your eye more than my drawing itself,
 which you won't look at. That's your choice,
 but isn't there more than a smudge between us?

(Artist crosses stage and centers himself behind an empty
window frame at the edge of stage closest to audience, so
that he is facing the audience, while nocturnal NYC footage
in rain appears on screen backdrop.)

 Out the window, on the avenue of art,
 even the cop directing traffic
 is drawing lines in the dark,
                         waving his flashlight.
 Art is everywhere, Beatrice—
 come look at the streets.

(Artist steps back from frame. Beatrice turns from the couch,
crosses to window frame and leans through same.)

BEATRICE:
 I see how cars claw through rain,
 pedestrians, metal trash cans
 brimming with broken umbrellas,
 awnings dripping, slick tires spinning
 lines defined out of water, glistening in yellow
 light a moment, then, by more rain—
                         undefined,
 like so much between us.

ARTIST:
 Surely you can see how things that resist
 definition have a way of lingering also,
 entering with the vocabulary of smoke, a breath,
 a tug of the lungs.

Beatrice, I know you're suspicious,
but there is and has always been only you.

BEATRICE:
You live in the world of imagination;
I hold to the actual, to the actual time you're away,
the actual arms of another that hold you to her.

You ask me to see art in our city,
but all I see is the blue-gray innuendo
in the haze hovering over a high-rise, and
then exiting through the gauze of fog.

(Turning from window to face Artist.)

I also see that we are two months behind in the rent.
Why don't you comb your precious streets
for an answer to that?

(Lights go down on center stage and spot hits stage right on Narrator.)

NARRATOR:
When he decided to take her advice and left,
she was standing, unnaturally still, stiff,
beside the window, perhaps watching drops of rain
steal down the pane, without registering
the skyline beyond.
                          Drink in hand, cigarette
sizzling—very film noir, might as well have been
a different decade—Beatrice looked like
she couldn't move, but was moved.

The time for saying something had passed.
The artist wasn't equipped with words—
syllables stalled at the palette, earth-staggering
weight of moment and momentum—he left,
remembering that earlier, happier time—
that first time she came to his home.

(Kill spot on Narrator and pull lights back up on Artist's apartment. Artist is alone, pacing. Knock at door. Artist crosses to door frame stage left, opens and Beatrice enters.)

ARTIST:
   Now that you've come to my home,
   different, as a thought, can finally
   surrender to the remote,
   and though I don't care about much,
   I know I don't want you to leave.
   But you're shivering; is it awful outside?

BEATRICE:
   The rain and wind began at noon today,
   picking up where last night left off.
   It's enough to leave anyone shivering.

ARTIST:
   Just now, your rap at the door
   was enough to start my hands
   traveling toward a drink,
   and now that you're with me,
   something more's throttling the engine in my chest.

   But perhaps I've said too much,
   I simply meant to ask if you want a drink.

(Beatrice turns her back to Artist, offers blush and smile to audience.)

BEATRICE:
   He's more articulate than most artists.
   I expected he'd reserve that for his canvas.

(Turning back to face Artist.)

   Yes, I'd love a drink,
   something strong to warm me.

*(Artist moves to cupboard, locates bottle and glasses,
while pouring drinks and bringing one to Beatrice,
sings with face forward to audience.)*

ARTIST:
   I'm not sure how much to let on I care,
   that her sudden presence challenges all.
   But when the door opened, it didn't seem to care
   about the color of her hair, the color of her eyes,
   the fullness of lips—and just maybe,
   I should take my lead from the door.

(Artist hands drink to Beatrice.)

   To what are we drinking?

BEATRICE:
   To the first meeting.

ARTIST:
   To the first meeting.

*(They clink their glasses then drink. During exchange below,
which deliberately plays on* La Bohème*'s "Che Gelida
Manina" aria, the music offers a nod to the allusion.)*

BEATRICE:
   So what are you anyway?

ARTIST:
   Me, I am an artist.

BEATRICE:
   How do you live? I mean, what do you do?

ARTIST:
   I live by painting.

(Lights go down on center stage and spot hits stage right on Narrator.)

NARRATOR:
   When Beatrice had first entered his apartment,
   she was standing, as he would later draw her,
   without an umbrella, locks of hair clinging to
   her forehead, wet-eyelashes, wings-fluttering—

   Meantime, the door opened on her—
   hinge holding hard to rust and wood,
   frame stiff with the stillness of stone—
   took in the stunning beauty of their uncertainty,
   of how little they knew what would happen next.

   But what happened was already set in stone:
   They both fell hard and fast,
   then she moved in and,
   before either noticed, months elapsed.

   And this all happened while he was busy on
   Manhattan in charcoal and, somehow,
   inexplicably, her suspicions were quiet
   and she still believed in his craft.

(Kill spot on Narrator.)

Movement 2

(Lights up on Artist and Beatrice at center stage embracing,
kissing, then Artist pulls away, paces while singing.)

ARTIST:
> Manhattan in charcoal is almost done,
> but it's so different than when I began.
> I saw it with paint, the brush was lifted,
> wet, glistening, poised with pigment,
> hovering above a stretched canvas,
> then it went to a work on paper.
> It was like learning to walk again—
> I might as well have been nine months old—
> weak legged on sticks, scribbling,
> then stumbling, falling, the precarious descent,
> then standing again, wobbly, perhaps drooling—
> I'd already primed the canvas with gesso.

(Artist stops pacing, turns back to Beatrice.)

BEATRICE:
> "Outsider Art" is what the man at the gallery
> called it, then suggested it would help to sell
> if we could say you'd spent some time in a hospital.

ARTIST:
> Me, I never needed a name for my efforts, just time.

BEATRICE:
> And time is what you'll have now if you finish.
> Let them call you an "Outsider."
> Hell, you can drool a bit,
> if only it'll move the work quicker.
> You know the way the Landlord leers at me.

ARTIST:
Keep your distance from him, girl.
He's more than just money on his mind.

(Lights go down on center stage and spot hits stage right on Narrator.)

NARRATOR:
But this was before the gallery showed his work,
before that woman approached the artist
at the show and spoke to him,
touched his arm and laughed in that way
Beatrice thought she understood,
even before Beatrice got a whiff of her,
recognized her scent.

That night, after Beatrice sent the artist packing
and he walked out, hit the streets,
from downstairs, he watched her, still standing
by the window. In the park across the street,
he stood before a statue of one founding father
or another who had a red circle A
for the Anarchist party spray painted on his chest.

And outside, standing by that statue,
The artist finally got it
how, sometimes, there's no pane to separate
the face from the elements, and in the mist
and streetlight, stone cheeks are left to glisten.

(Spot goes down at stage right on Narrator and another pulls up extreme stage left on Artist under streetlight, alone on sidewalk.)

ARTIST:
A busy sidewalk is a scribble of intersecting lines.
Things moving and still tend to blend and blur,

rubbing, as they do, against negative space.
Tonight, the city that never sleeps is lulled, medicated,
sawing wood in tangled sheets, ready to be drawn.

*(Reduce brightness of spot on Artist but leave him visible,
then bring up another spot on Beatrice alone in loft set center
stage.)*

BEATRICE:
    I once asked him how he saw art
    all over the place and—
    (I genuinely wanted to understand him)—
    at the time, he had no answer;
    tongue-tied, he finally said
    he couldn't explain
    a function as natural as breathing.

*(Reduce brightness of spot on Beatrice but leave her visible,
then bring back up full the other spot on Artist back at stage
right.)*

ARTIST:
    She once asked me to explain
    how I see things the way I do.
    What could I say?
    Of course, there's certainly no advantage to
    the hyper-focused lens, but I wouldn't
    change a thing on that score.

    Only thing I would change would be to learn
    how to talk with her without the throat-clench,
    dry-wood, kindling caught and coughing,
    bashful, bruised-self business of it all.

*(Reduce brightness of spot on Artist but leave him visible,
then bring back up full the other spot on Beatrice back at
center stage.)*

BEATRICE:

That first night, somehow we spoke easily
of childhood and family, as if
one of us could offer the other insight,
or might've been a friendly Freudian,
not too disenchanted to appreciate sex for sex.

And at first, I liked being with an artist.

(Leave spot on Beatrice during duet while also having another spot on Artist back at stage right.)

BEATRICE AND ARTIST:

It was "exciting"
to live with the process.
And back then, as if by accident,
we had money.
We celebrated the city,
celebrated Manhattan in charcoal.
And after we went through the money,
drank our way through the dollars,
we were still invincible.

(Lose spot on Artist and dim light on Beatrice but leave her visible, as light now also shows Narrator visible back at stage left.)

NARRATOR:

When they'd gone through the money
earmarked for canvases and paint—
umbers and cadmiums—
the artist was left working with paper and charcoal.

But he looked the other way, even when
he knew what was coming,
months before Beatrice
started to feel the pinch of them
suddenly being broke again.

BEATRICE:

He thought I cared about the money—
damn, somebody has to—
but that wasn't it, not all anyway.
I watched him struggle; I knew
there was more to the game at play.

NARRATOR:

Prior to finding the one damn place
that would show the Artist's work,
what the galleries wanted was
performance pieces that made the audience
part of the composition,
or for those that still moved actual pieces,
if it was brushwork, and not silk-screen,
they wanted thin acrylics.
Each buyer had their own absurd view
that always came down to
whatever they thought
might make the most money.

Movement 3

(Art Dealers emerge from wings stage right.)

ART DEALER 1:
Please, dear, let it be a pretty landscape
that will fit neatly over a couch.

ART DEALER 2:
Oh please, if it must be abstract, let it be
a neutral monotone work that will get along
with a wide assortment of colors.

ART DEALER 3:
Please, if you must texture the canvas
with a palette knife, don't go so primitive
you'll scare away buyers.

(Art Dealers 1, 2 and 3 now as chorus together:)

Whatever you do, don't try
finding yourself or doing anything
too dreadfully new and different.

Just give me something that will sell.
Oh, something that will sell would be lovely,
such a refreshing change—
you've no idea how fickle buyers can be.

Put yourself in my shoes,
I need works that will sell.
Oh, yes, that's it exactly—
just give me something that will sell.

That's a good boy, good artist, nice artist—

please, let your precious aesthetics go to Hell
and just get me what will sell.

(Lights down stage right and pull up on stage left.)

NARRATOR:
Last thing they wanted was a work on paper,
an urban study in charcoal, but that was all he could
afford to work in by then and, anyway, he rationalized
what he longed for was something uncomplicated—
simplicity rendering every street into one
without forgetting or forgiving a single shadow,
simplicity as chewable as the syllables uttered in a poem,
simplicity as stark as our city itself.

(Lights down stage left and pull up on stage right.)

ARTIST:
When I started to draw Manhattan in charcoal,
it was winter and in the earliest sketches,
brownstones shrugged in pebbles of gray snow,
crusting at corniced shoulders.
        Snow drifts presented instant sculptures.
Outside, the wind was wheezing, lungs constricting.
The voice was looking for a hole to crawl into.
When I walked through the village,
I longed for simplicity, something to clear my head.
Meantime, my teeth chattering
kept time with my clicking feet—
I might as well have been a nineteenth-century
consumptive, no doubt art critics would love that;
artists always fare better with another century's edge.

I knew what Beatrice wanted—
the exhilaration of a first love,
to be inexplicably young, amorous and amazed all over.
But in a storm's scribbled sketch,
all I could offer her was my drawing,
my scratches at the city we both knew so well.

109

(Lights down stage right and pull up on center stage mini gallery scene where people mill about. At center facing audience, a ten foot by ten foot work of Manhattan in charcoal. When Artist enters from stage right, crowd applauds and surrounds him.)

ARTIST:
Thank you one and all.
There are no words . . .

ART CRITIC:
Why yes, there are always words.
As a critic here to review your opening,
I've a few that come to mind:

The tortured extremis contained in the
profound tension of each line reflects on
the very content this work is considering,
namely, the tense and tortured city of New York.

ARTIST: *(turning to attractive young woman who appears at his side, sotto voce)*
But I wasn't thinking any of that.
It's just the way I draw.

(Young woman holds onto Artist's arm, giggling.)

ART CRITIC:
What's that you're saying?

ARTIST:
It's just the way it's raw—

ART CRITIC:
What?

ARTIST:
   Just like Manhattan perhaps—
   exposed and raw—
   but you know how to put it best.

(Art Critic looks at Artist, sizing him up, then turns away, just as Beatrice enters gallery and observes Artist with young woman.)

BEATRICE:
   The way that girl
   holds onto his arm,
   whispers in his ear and giggles,
   as if something brilliant
   has just passed between them,
   it's plain as day she wants to play.

   And now, when he sees me seeing them,
   the way he offers his shoulder-drop,
   limp and sour lip-twist smile,
   mutters to the girl, and then
   she removes her hand from his arm,
   pulls back her shoulders,
   puffs up her chest in perfect
   battle posture.

   I know what she's about at a glance.
   I don't need to see anymore.

(Beatrice exits stage left, lights go down.)

Movement 4

(Spot comes up on Beatrice in Artist's home studio tearing up Artist's drawings and trashing studio in a frenzy.)

BEATRICE:
> So much for your precious art,
> your goddamned, insightful suffering.
> You want suffering?
> I'll show you suffering.
>
> You once told me you were,
> if nothing else, at least an honest man.
> But where is there one honest man,
> one remotely sincere artist worth his salt?
>
> Just an honest man,
> that's all I wanted—
> an honest man who might understand—

(Spot goes down at stage left on Beatrice and another pulls up extreme stage right on Artist under streetlight, on sidewalk.)

ARTIST:
> I had to get away from the gallery;
> my head's still spinning.
> It seems the work was well received;
> I might even have a few dollars in the end.
>
> But Beatrice saw me with her.
> It was nothing, of course,
> a momentary exchange at a show.
> It's all theater, all gestures and
> eye contact across a room.

What can any of it mean?
Of course, Beatrice can't be really upset.

Only now, walking alone again across my city,
can a man get a measure on how things stand.

In this darkness, interrupted by occasional neon,
shadows bend, multiply and win.
The wet wind, delivering horizontal rain,
has a wild temper that makes me
shiver slightly and think of Beatrice.

In our city, every fear that can
cripple two people together, generally does.
Despite this, I'm still walking, the feet are
propelled, still pounding pavement, still sketching
shoeprints in the rain-slicked sidewalk.

In this darkness, steps interrupt thoughts of
her at home, perhaps standing by the window,
steps measure breaths between avenues,
steps measure the feet closer to our bed,
steps measure a future where the exiled Prince
returns, beaten and beard-white—
though love's brittle as a tree's frozen twigs.

*(Lights down on Artist stage right and pull up on Beatrice
stage left, back in Artist's home studio off living room set,
facing audience.)*

BEATRICE:
It all started with him liking to walk alone
in the dark, just as I suppose he is right now.
I'd be wired on the floor by the fire
with my Want warming to an impulse.
Next, we'd play with words, kindling, flames.
I'd listen to the warble in his throat,

recognize his cough, recognize his
need to remain remote.

Questions like—
Is there someone else?
lined up neatly in my head and throbbed.

After that, what would be left to speak about
when a chair moving could utter something
too loud?
            We'd lie on the carpeted floor
feeling our clouds, study every inch of ceiling,
then grope, gradually, in the dark to find
that smoldering thing that might still be kind.

I can't say why, after we groaned and wrestled
for as long as it took, and sometimes more,
when he stood up, I'd follow him to the corridor,
still unable to call the moment complete,
inanely staring at his legs and feet.

*(Lights lower stage left but leave Beatrice barely visible
while spot finds Artist stage right facing toward stage left.)*

ARTIST:
Words stop short, lips dry, throat parched,
when memories traverse the parquet floor
where we've lived and loved and more—
it's here I forget what I meant to follow,
meant to do and, feeling hollow, sometimes
decide I like the look of a deserted street—
my steps marked briefly in puddles,
like a child splashing down a sidewalk
longing to learn something from anything
or merely to let off steam—
but then I always return to you, Beatrice,
return to find you between the sheets.

What can I say? Sometimes I need a street—
but forgive me Beatrice for loitering so long
at the tall door of your heart.
Anyway, as the saying goes,
man ain't Beethoven and maybe
the little bit left I do know, at times,
boils down, between your thighs,
to the fear of being alone with my own sighs.

(Lights down on Artist and pull back full to Beatrice.)

BEATRICE:
Now that I've destroyed his art,
just as he's destroyed me,
I feel lighter, as if anything's possible.
But hush my troubled self and all,
I hear him in the hall.

(Enter Artist, crossing through living room to his studio. Picks up shredded canvas, torn works on paper.)

ARTIST: *(sotto voce)*
My God, what have you done?
Do you really hate me this much?

(Artist grabs Beatrice and shakes her shoulders, raising his voice.)

What the hell's wrong with you?
Do you know what you've done?

BEATRICE:
I saw her.

ARTIST: *(Letting go of Beatrice, steps back.)*
Who?

BEATRICE:
The girl.

ARTIST:
What girl?

BEATRICE:
The one hanging on your arm
at the gallery,
clinging to you as if glued there.

ARTIST:
She's nobody, a young admirer.

Beatrice, you've destroyed my work—
this is insanity!
You know how long this work took,
how much it means to me,
and now you're talking rubbish.
There's no being with you—
I'm leaving.

BEATRICE:
To go to her?

ARTIST:
No, of course not. There is no her.

BEATRICE:
You know, she will never love you the way I do.
She will never understand you the way I do.

You don't have to lie.

Haven't we always said
we can tell each other anything?

Artist: *(Back to picking up the art Beatrice destroyed, Artist suddenly drops destroyed artwork and turns to Beatrice.)*

You want the truth?

Fine.
Yes, I am going to her,
but just this one last time.

I promise you, Beatrice,
just one last time.

Is that what you wanted to hear?
Now will you give me a moment's peace?

BEATRICE:
Don't do this to us,
Don't leave me.

ARTIST:
I must.

BEATRICE:
But why?

ARTIST: *(Staring at floor.)*
She's pregnant.

BEATRICE:
What? Pregnant!

Haven't I always told you,
no one can love you the way I do?

ARTIST:
You have, and I know it's true.

BEATRICE:
Then stay, don't go to her.

(Recalling verses from earlier in the libretto with same music, she sings through tears.)

It was "exciting"
to live with the process...

We celebrated the city,
celebrated Manhattan in charcoal...

We were still invincible.

ARTIST:
But I must go.

BEATRICE:
Why?

ARTIST:
She's agreed to an abortion.
She's agreed to end it all.
I promised I'd go with her.

Just wait for me here.
We'll get past this,
put it all behind us.

(Artist exits.)

BEATRICE: *(Again lifting language from earlier with same music.)*
But there is and has always been only you.
But there is and has always been only you.

(Beatrice looks to where Artist just left, then crosses to Artist's table covered with brushes, palette, etc., and lifts up a bottle

of turpentine, stares at it.)

Here's your precious turpentine,
that's used to diminish color, clean brushes,
and mediate the art you've lived by.
But art can also bring one to die.

*(Beatrice raises bottle of turpentine. Lines below from earlier
return with earlier music.)*

To what are we drinking?

To the first meeting.

*(Beatrice drinks the bottle of turpentine then collapses. Lights
down on Beatrice then up on Artist walking through city.)*

ARTIST:
Now the deed is done,
I can return to my home,
make peace with Beatrice,
and life will move on.

But walking through town in the rain,
I'm still thinking of the child that almost was,
though I try, take steps, and more steps each block,
to erase the bleak image from my head.

A scream nearby sounds like an argument,
while an ambulance's siren, bending
its note as it turns a corner, supports the position—
but that's too musical when what's needed are
clean lines, or filthy lines, charcoal rubbed over
with the thumb, or at least someone with
a good heart for the screamer.

Let's say Beatrice is still at home,
even waiting for me, no longer

staring by the window,
eyes glassy as the wet glass itself.

And what if it's decided I've gotten it right,
drawn a Manhattan of mind and gut,
sketched the beloved stretched as a skyscraper,
or captured the inconsistent architecture
of the torso of my town—

And what if, now that I've sold the piece to
a blind arbiter of new works,
Beatrice reads some drivel
about my tormented textures
in a learned magazine.
Will it be enough?

It's dawn now. The rain is finally letting up.
And as the night's familiar black sheet is ripped—
a finger's last rub from a black carved stick—
first light's colors glide in with departing clouds.

And as I walk home, retracing my steps
through this city that holds and is held to
its own palette, this city brought from a myth
into something some of us are lucky enough
to actually live with, I'm alone with one wish,
that I might find Beatrice still in our loft.

*(Lights down on sidewalk mini-scene then up stage left on
studio off living room, where Beatrice is still collapsed on
floor. Artist enters, crosses to Beatrice and drops to his knees
beside her.)*

No! Please, you can't be gone.
I can't lose you.
The hell with my art,
the hell with New York city.
I curse it all.

I see now:
art without love is nothing.
I'm sorry Beatrice.
Please, speak to me.

(Artist bends over and kisses Beatrice, who then starts coughing.)

BEATRICE:
Fool of an artist,
I'm not gone.
I did try,
but only succeeded in getting myself sick,
then passed out here.

For an artist, you understand so little.
Don't you know, in New York
the challenge is not dying,
the challenge is living.

(Lights out.)